TEACHING

FOR

CRIMINAL

JUSTICE

PROFESSIONALS

**THE
INSIDERS
STEP-BY-STEP GUIDE
TO LANDING A
TEACHING JOB AT
A COLLEGE OR
UNIVERSITY**

KELLY WILLIAM ENOS

Skydog Press

Teaching for Criminal Justice Professionals

ISBN: 979-8-218-45569-9 Paperback

ISBN: 979-8-218-45570-5 eBook

The mediocre teacher tells.
The good teacher explains.
The superior teacher demonstrates.
The great teacher inspires.

– William A. Ward

TABLE OF CONTENTS

Chapter 1 | 1
Introduction

Chapter 2 | 7
Why Should You Teach Part-time Classes
in Administration of Justice?

Chapter 3 | 15
Teaching Credit and Noncredit Classes

Chapter 4 | 19
Where to Find Positions

Chapter 5 | 21
Instructor Qualifications for Community
Colleges and Universities

Chapter 6 | 27
Advisory Boards, Networking, and Guest Speakers

Chapter 7 | 29
Resume/CV/Cover Letters

Chapter 8 | 31
Presentations and Trade Associations

Chapter 9 | 35
Teaching Internships

Chapter 10 | 37
Academic Search and Hiring Committees

Chapter 11 | 39
The Application and Job Interview
for an Instructor Position

Chapter 12 | 45
Quick Tips for Landing an Instructor Position

Conclusion | 50

Glossary | 51

Websites | 53

Additional Resources | 55

CHAPTER 1

INTRODUCTION

HAVE YOU EVER wondered what it would be like to teach a criminal justice course at a community college or university or to stand in front of thirty or more students describing a case that you were recently involved in? Or maybe you thought about supplementing your income with a part-time job that could provide both a steady stream of work and value to others. If those apply to you, and I think they do or you wouldn't have bought this book, you have come to the right place.

In this book, I describe the process and best practices for obtaining a part-time instructor position at a college or university in the discipline of administration of justice.

For years as I worked as a full-time administration of justice instructor and acting dean of academic affairs, I served on many hiring committees. I saw many applicants come through the hiring process who were not prepared to teach at the community college level. It was disappointing to devote so much time and energy interviewing candidates and then in the end not choose anyone because no one had the experience or education to teach. In some cases, we didn't even have enough qualified applicants to interview, and it became a failed search.

When we *were* able to hire an adjunct administration of justice instructor, we would evaluate them during the first semester of teaching, only to find that the new hire was a poor instructor and not willing to improve. While we did ultimately find several applicants who were great instructors, many were not, and we let them go after only one semester.

There is a critical need for instructors in criminal justice programs who are educated not only in their fields of study but also in how to teach at the community college and university level. I always wished that there was a way to make potential applicants aware of the ways to prepare to become a part-time instructor at the community college and university level but never had the chance to do so myself—until now.

I wrote this book with the intent to help criminal justice professionals prepare for a part-time career teaching administration of justice classes at a college or university. Having seen so many applicants disqualified for incomplete applications or poor interviews, I wanted to share my experiences and demonstrate how to successfully get a job teaching at a college or university.

My interest in teaching goes back to my early days of attending community college right out of high school and taking criminal justice courses. Off-duty police officers or deputy sheriffs taught many of the courses, and after a while, I grew to love the idea of someday teaching a college class on a subject I had a deep passion for.

When I was taking administration of justice classes at West Los Angeles College, the instructor was a deputy sheriff with the Los Angeles County Sheriff's Department. He was teaching an evening class, and I thought at that time that I would like to teach a criminal justice class like him someday. Later in my career, I attended in-service training workshops and seminars that were taught by excellent instructors and often hoped to do the same.

After taking an early retirement from the sheriff's department, I started teaching traffic school in the evenings (more on this later). The pay was not great, but it gave me several years of experience teaching a variety of adults. I was able to try different approaches and techniques, and I was comforted that I had a captive audience; they had to stay for eight hours to get their certification. As the years rolled by, more and more attendees gave me feedback on my teaching ability and encouraged me to take it to the next level—community college teaching.

I had no idea how to apply or find out how to teach at a community college. I did what most people probably do; I started cold calling. I called the Administration of Justice Department at Los Angeles Mission College and talked with the department chair who encouraged me to send him a resume. Just a few months later, I received a call and a request to teach a course during the upcoming semester. It was that simple.

During that time, the college did not require hiring committees for adjunct instructors. Department chairs were authorized to hire adjuncts at their discretion. As of this writing, that practice has changed, and adjunct instructor applicants go through the standard application process and interview. More on that later.

In 2003, I graduated from California State University, Los Angeles, with my Master's degree in Criminal Justice Administration. Approximately two years later, my graduate advisor called to ask if I would be interested in coming back to the university as a part-time lecturer. I was surprised at the offer and felt honored that he would think of me as a great lecturer in the department. I jumped at the chance and started teaching part-time. I taught every quarter and semester for the next sixteen years.

In 2007, I was hired as a full-time instructor in the Administration of Justice Program at Los Angeles Mission College and have been there ever since. My duties include overseeing the program, hiring part-time instructors, forming advisory boards, evaluating instructors, updating curricula, and scheduling.

I wish to share with you tips and suggestions for entering a part-time career teaching criminal justice classes at institutions of higher learning. It is a noble profession where we teach and mentor the next generation of young adults seeking a career in the criminal justice system—a system that needs talented, educated, and highly motivated people to make it work. It has been a rewarding experience for me throughout the years, and I know it can be for you too. Let's get started.

"Education is the key to success in life, and teachers make a lasting impact in the lives of their students."

–Solomon Ortiz

CHAPTER 2

WHY SHOULD YOU TEACH PART-TIME CLASSES IN ADMINISTRATION OF JUSTICE?

TEACHING A COLLEGE class is fun. Students are taking the class because they have a deep interest in the criminal justice system, are hungry for information, and want to learn from people who have worked in the system. They want to look up to their instructors as role models. Most criminal justice instructors at the community college level have a full-time day job in some area of criminal justice and teach part-time. It can supplement a regular job. It is possible, for instance, to work as a prosecutor or defense attorney during the day and teach a course at night or to work as a police officer during an early morning shift and teach a class after work.

Many classes are now taught online, which allows an instructor to engage with students at any time of the day or night. Teaching online can also be done from anywhere in the country. Some instructors live out of state from where they teach and never set foot on the campus. All you need is access to the internet.

Criminal Justice programs offer a wide range of courses depending on the college or university, giving you many course options to teach. Below are just a few of them:

Introduction to Administration of Justice
Concepts of Criminal Law
Criminal Evidence
Criminal Investigation

Report Writing
Domestic Violence
Introduction to Corrections
Juvenile Procedures
Probation and Parole
Forensics
Ethics in Criminal Justice
Criminological Theory

According to the Association for Career and Technical Education, there are many other reasons to teach college courses including:

1. Making a difference in your community. Administration of justice instructors are in a unique position to teach and develop the next generation of criminal justice practitioners and impact the lives of countless individuals and families.

2. All of us got into the criminal justice system to make a difference in our communities. Share that same passion by teaching others about the career you love.

3. Prepare students for the real world. Students have a great deal of respect for instructors who have been there, done that, and don't just teach in theoretical terms or themes. Criminal Justice instructors know how the real world works and share that with their students.

4. Criminal Justice instructors are in the position to motivate and engage students to be their best. Often, just sharing our personal stories

with them and how we started our careers can be motivating for students.

5. Part-time instructors typically have a work or teaching schedule that allows them time off during the holidays and over the summer, making time for family.

6. Earn good pay and benefits. Some community colleges and universities offer benefit packages to part-time instructors, including medical, dental, and retirement benefits. Part-time instructors can make anywhere from $5,000 to $15,000 per semester depending on the number of classes they teach. The hourly range is from $60 to $96 per hour.

7. Job Security. There is a wide variety of positions available throughout the country, including at community colleges, public and private universities, and technical skills centers. Many colleges and public universities have labor contract agreements giving part-time instructors certain rights to assignments.

8. Enjoy variety. Criminal Justice programs include a wide range of classes, including criminal evidence, criminal investigation, forensics, policing, probation, corrections, and criminal law.

9. Be a life-long learner. Instructors have access to professional development opportunities to improve their teaching skills in their subject areas. In some cases, part-time instructors can

also move into leadership roles at the institution.

Other benefits include flexible hours and classes that are offered on different days and times, many of which are online.

Peace Officers who also work as instructors have limited exposure to civil liability. Many officers work off-duty jobs in security or personal protection that may expose them to civil liability. As a result, some departments require officers to get permission to work off-duty jobs if they entail potentially making arrests or using force. Teaching at a community college or university eliminates those risks.

Now that I have shared with you why you should consider teaching as a part-time instructor, let's take a look in Chapter 3 at the different kinds of classes that are available.

"Tell me and I forget, teach me and I may remember, involve me and I learn."

-Benjamin Franklin

TEACHING CREDIT AND NONCREDIT CLASSES

THE TERMS "ADMINISTRATION of justice" and "criminal justice" are used interchangeably in this book. Generally speaking, the term "administration of justice" is used at the community college level, and "criminal justice" is used at the university level.

There are two major categories of courses available at colleges and universities: credit and noncredit. Credit classes are those that can be applied to a degree or certificate if the student successfully passes the class. These credit classes are what most college instructors teach during their assignments. The credits earned can often be transferred to a four-year university.

Noncredit classes are different and provide additional teaching opportunities for instructors. Let's first define what they are and how they can provide additional opportunities to teach college classes.

Noncredit classes are free to students and are useful

alternatives to credit options for students who do not qualify for financial aid. Noncredit courses can be open entry/open exit, which means that students come and go as they please, sometimes attending all course sessions or just attending those portions that apply to them. For other types of noncredit classes, students must attend all of the sessions to successfully finish. These kinds of noncredit courses benefit adult students with busy work schedules, family responsibilities, and other obligations. Noncredit classes and programs can also provide short and targeted instruction to meet students' professional development needs. The fact that noncredit courses focus on skills attainment and are repeatable can help underrepresented students build confidence and gain both cognitive and noncognitive skills that are necessary for success in credit courses.

In addition, noncredit courses provide entry-level career technical certificates and accessible entry points to various career and academic pathways.

Noncredit classes provide the same quality of instruction as credit classes. While noncredit courses are not applicable toward a degree or transfer, upon successful completion of a series of two or more required classes, students can sometimes earn a noncredit certificate of completion or competency. Noncredit classes can also lead directly to employment. These noncredit classes are additional opportunities for part-time instructors to teach a wide variety of topics.

Let's take Santa Barbara City College as an example. On their website, they list dozens of noncredit professional development classes offered through the Career

Skills Institute of the School of Extended Learning. Below is just a sample of the many classes they offer each semester:

- Leadership Skills
- Successfully Managing and Developing People
- Supervisory Skills
- Workplace Politics

Some of these classes are taught over a one or two-day period and are offered online, in-person, or via Zoom. The skills for teaching a noncredit class are no different than for teaching a credit class, and both count as experience teaching in higher education.

In the next chapter, we will look at where to find part-time teaching opportunities across the country.

CHAPTER 4

WHERE TO FIND POSITIONS

SOME PART-TIME ADMINISTRATION of justice teaching positions are advertised, and some are not. The manner of attracting candidates depends on the college, university, or state.

One of the first places to start is with a state's registry system. In California, the California Community Colleges Registry lists open full-time and part-time academic positions for the entire state. Their website makes it easy to find open positions and apply. In Nevada, it would be the Nevada System of Higher Education website.

Professional Associations are another good place to look for posted teaching positions, and many list job openings on their websites. Below are a few examples:

- International Association for Identification
- Academy of Criminal Justice Sciences
- The Chronicle of Higher Education

Academic teaching jobs can also be found on pay sites,

including FlexJobs, which lists part-time and fully remote college teaching jobs throughout the United States and other countries.

There are also part-time positions that are not advertised, such as the one that Cal State L.A. offered me. Because some positions are not advertised, it is important to network with as many people in academia as you can. If you are going back to school to earn your college degree in criminal justice, get to know the department chair and make it known that you are interested in teaching a college course someday.

Make yourself available to guest speak in an administration of justice class or serve as an advisory board member for the program.

Now that you know where to look for open positions, which qualifications are required to teach at a community college or university? That is the subject of the next chapter.

CHAPTER 5

INSTRUCTOR QUALIFICATIONS FOR COMMUNITY COLLEGES AND UNIVERSITIES

IN CALIFORNIA, THE minimum requirements to teach criminal justice or vocational classes at the community college level for both credit and noncredit classes are possession of an Associate's Degree and six years of professional experience or possession of a Bachelor's Degree and two years of professional experience.

Professional experience is defined as working in a full-time position that is directly related to the faculty member's teaching assignment. For example, if a deputy sheriff earned a Bachelor's Degree and worked at least two years in custody and patrol assignments, he or she would be eligible to teach most criminal justice courses.

Does working as a reserve peace officer count as professional experience? It depends. Some colleges or universities define "professional experience" as "full-time work." Reserve officers are typically part-time volunteers and therefore may not be eligible. It would depend upon the college/university or state education codes.

For Maricopa Community Colleges in Arizona, the minimum requirements to teach administration of justice courses are a Bachelor's Degree and three years of occupational experience working in the criminal justice system.

Austin Texas Community Colleges require a Bachelor's Degree in Criminal Justice or a related field or a Master's Degree with eighteen graduate hours in Criminal Justice or a related field or an Associate's Degree in Criminal Justice or a related field and three years of non-teaching work experience.

Keep in mind that these are minimum requirements that colleges list in their job announcements.

The following list of criminal justice occupations may also make one eligible to teach criminal justice courses:

- F.B.I. Agent
- Secret Service Agent
- Probation Officer
- Forensic Scientist or Criminalist
- Prosecutor
- Public Defender
- Parole Officer
- Investigator with California Alcohol and Beverage Control
- Investigator with the Department of Motor Vehicles
- Special Agent with the California Department of Justice
- Crime Analyst

- Coroner Investigator
- Drug Enforcement Administration Special Agent
- ATF Agent
- Customs and Border Protection Officer
- State and/or Federal Criminal Investigator
- Crime Scene Technician
- Police Officer
- Deputy Sheriff
- Border Patrol Officer
- California Correctional Officer
- Deputy U.S. Marshall
- Judge

Some teaching positions require graduate degrees. I highly recommend earning a Master's Degree to be more marketable to both community colleges and universities. Some community colleges pay those with doctorates even more.

For most universities, the minimum requirement to teach undergraduate classes is a Master's Degree and some professional experience. In California, part-time instructors are typically referred to as lecturers and teach criminal justice classes much the same as they would be taught at a community college.

"Desirable qualifications" are included in job announcements and outline skillsets that would make a more desirable candidate to teach administration of justice classes. These may vary from one college to another.

Below are some desirable qualifications that might be found in a job announcement:

- Possession of a Master's Degree or higher in Criminal Justice or a closely related field.
- Instructional experience in a broad range of subjects within the criminal justice discipline at the post-secondary level.
- Knowledge of the development and assessment of student learning outcomes.
- Knowledge and use of current education technology methods and tools.
- Demonstrated positive interpersonal skills.
- Ability to instruct students with a wide variety of learning styles using various successful teaching techniques, including creating innovative academic learning environments.
- Exceptionally strong organizational and problem-solving skills.
- Ability to plan, establish priorities, and handle multiple tasks and projects.
- Learner-centered focus with a demonstrated sensitivity and ability to inspire, motivate, and empower students to succeed.
- Exceptional oral presentation and written communication skills.
- Demonstrated ability to provide dynamic instruction based on various teaching modalities.
- Experience and sensitivity working with a diverse student body population and community.
- Demonstrated ability to develop and assess student learning objectives.

- Demonstrate a willingness to serve on committees with the department and college.
- Evidence of certification to teach online classes.

One of the most important things to do is attain certification to teach online, what is referred to as asynchronous classes. An asynchronous class is defined as a class that is taught online where there are no meetings between the instructor and students. Synchronous classes are defined as where there are class sessions where the instructor meets face-to-face with students either in-person or via Zoom meetings. Asynchronous classes are placed on an online platform that students can access and where they can complete coursework at any time—24/7. Online classes last five, twelve, or—traditionally—sixteen weeks. There are deadlines for assignments and exams; however, students can complete the work anytime during the day or week. Online classes have become more popular with students since the COVID-19 pandemic and are in great demand across the country. There are many benefits for instructors and they include:

1. Teaching from anywhere. There are many faculty who teach online for a college in one state and live in another. This could work for international classes as well.
2. Flexible hours. You can teach the class from the comfort of your home or even if you are traveling, teaching the class at any hour of the day or night.
3. Many online platforms are set up to automati-

cally correct exams and make it easier to correct papers and discussion assignments.

4. Spending more time with family at home but still taking on part-time work.

There are many educational online platforms such as Moodle, Blackboard, and Canvas. Canvas is a popular online platform that is used in several community colleges in California as well as the California State University system.

Being certified as an online instructor makes a candidate more marketable across the country. However, not all administration of justice instructors are certified in online teaching, and it is not for everyone. Some instructors who have been teaching for a long time prefer in-person classes and would never teach an online course. Teaching online is a different experience for both instructors and students.

As a new online instructor, you would need to create a class shell online to prepare for the semester, which includes creating a syllabus, tests, lectures, assignments, discussions, and handouts. Creating a class online for the first time is a lot of work but, once finished, can be used again for the next semester with a few modifications.

Let's now take a look at additional ways to meet people in academia and start a teaching career.

CHAPTER 6

ADVISORY BOARDS, NETWORKING, AND GUEST SPEAKERS

CONGRESS PASSED THE federal Carl D. Perkins Career Technical Education Improvement Act to provide funding to colleges and universities to improve career-technical education programs, including administration of justice or criminal justice programs. As part of the requirements for receiving funding, colleges must involve representatives from a particular business area or industry to evaluate their career technical education programs, such as criminal justice. This typically involves forming an advisory committee that meets at least twice a year. Program directors or department chairs look for industry experts to serve on the board for at least one year.

The time commitment for a board member is minimal, and the size of the board varies greatly. I have seen boards with over twenty members and others with as few as eight. Board members volunteer their time to serve and provide valuable feedback to evaluate the program and see if it is meeting the needs of the industry.

One of the ways to get a foot in the door and meet the director or chair of a criminal justice department is to volunteer to serve on the board. Even though the board might meet only once or twice a year, it is a good idea to keep in touch with the director of the program and offer whatever assistance possible, such as guest speaking, providing equipment, or offering tours of a police building, courtroom or jail. An advisory board member might be able to provide resources to the program or department that they would normally not have access to.

Serving as an advisory board member offers exposure not only to the department chair but also to others who serve on the board. It is not unusual for the dean of the area to also attend the meetings.

Offering to be a guest speaker is also a great way to network with department chairs, vice chairs, and full-time instructors who typically have the authority to hire part-time instructors. Simply cold calling and sending emails or letters to department chairs offering to guest speak might be enough to earn an invitation. The more guest speaker engagements, the more exposure to the department.

Let's turn now to preparing a resume and cover letter.

CHAPTER 7

RESUME/CV/COVER LETTERS

WHAT IS THE difference between a resume and a CV, and which is preferred when applying for a faculty teaching position?

A resume will normally include all professional work or positions held for at least the past ten years. It should also include educational background and specific skill sets.

A CV, or "Curriculum Vitae," is normally preferred when applying to institutions of higher learning. It is similar to a resume but focuses on experience and education as they apply to the teaching position. For part-time teaching positions, either format is acceptable. For vocational disciplines, like criminal justice, it is important to indicate whether the referenced professional experience is part-time or full-time and include dates of employment.

Cover Letters

Hiring committees often ask for cover letters, or letters

of intent, in addition to a resume. The purpose of a cover letter is to elaborate in more detail on what is listed in the resume. It is written in narrative form and sometimes will include an applicant's teaching philosophy. Cover letters should be no more than one page in length. When describing current or former positions held at an agency, it is important to indicate whether it was full-time or part-time work.

Letters should be personalized to the institution and demonstrate knowledge of the program and a deliberate approach to getting a teaching position. Too often, we have seen cover letters that are generic and not addressed to any specific individuals or for any specific position. This sometimes conveys a lack of care and intent. Personalizing a cover letter can show you have done your homework and set you apart from other applicants.

CHAPTER 8

PRESENTATIONS AND TRADE ASSOCIATIONS

Presentations/Trainings

DURING YOUR CAREER, take advantage of opportunities to provide training workshops or presentations and list those in your resume. Even though your resume may not indicate you have taught *college courses,* it will still demonstrate teaching experience.

Many communities offer classes through their recreation departments or adult schools. These classes are typically targeted at people who would like to learn new skills, such as music, sports, computer applications, or hobbies. They are always looking for instructors to teach these classes, and the days and times for class meetings are usually flexible.

I started my teaching career by teaching traffic school, which gave me the experience to prepare me for my academic teaching career.

Many states, such as Nevada, California, Tennessee,

and Colorado, offer both in-person and online traffic school for people who have received a traffic ticket and would like to keep it from affecting their driving record and car insurance premiums. In Los Angeles County, California, alone, there are approximately thirty-six traffic schools that provide in-person classes. Classes are either four or eight hours long, and instructors teach the course based on state-approved curricula. Classes are sometimes offered in the evenings, twice a week, or all day on Saturdays. When I was teaching traffic school, I had tremendous freedom in how to deliver the course material, and it gave me experience speaking in front of groups of people not associated with the criminal justice system.

The requirements for landing a job teaching traffic school vary from state to state. In California, I first needed to be sponsored by a traffic school before I could take a certification test at the Department of Motor Vehicles. Next, I applied to the Department of Motor Vehicles and took a written examination. Once I passed, I became state-certified and could teach at any traffic school in California.

I taught traffic school classes for approximately five years and gained a lot of hands-on experience teaching adults and trying different teaching techniques to see what worked and what didn't. At the end of the classes, I would survey the class and ask for any feedback on my teaching ability so that I could improve.

Teaching traffic school was one of the best experiences of my life to prepare me for a career in academia and to later provide training classes for criminal justice professionals.

The main point I'm making is the importance of exposure to as many teaching opportunities as possible. Every opportunity offers the ability to meet and network with folks and practice teaching skills. You never know who might be in the audience asking to meet after class to discuss another teaching opportunity at another venue.

Trade Associations

Consider becoming a member of associations that promote teaching and training practices. Many out there invite members to give presentations or training sessions at their annual conferences. Often, they will advertise on their websites dates when they are accepting conference presentation proposals. The below associations and organizations are just a sample of what is out there:

- International Law Enforcement Educators and Trainers Association (ILEETA)
- International Association of Chiefs of Police (IACP)
- International Association of Directors of Law Enforcement (IADLEST)
- Academy of Criminal Justice Sciences (ACJS)

CHAPTER 9

TEACHING INTERNSHIPS

SOME COLLEGES OFFER internship opportunities to individuals who have no teaching experience but would like to teach college classes. One such program is Project Match at the Los Angeles Community College District. The program has been in place since the 1990s.

The purpose of the program is to prepare and recruit new faculty to serve as instructors at particular colleges. Participants apply to the program and, if selected, are assigned to a college campus in the discipline of their expertise.

They are then mentored by an adjunct or full-time faculty instructor for one semester. During that semester, the intern shadows the instructor to learn teaching techniques, classroom management, college administrative processes, and college culture. At some point in the semester, the intern will teach a small segment of the class and then receive feedback from the instructor. Interns must commit to working with their mentor approximately three hours per week for fifteen weeks.

In addition, interns complete two Canvas certification courses to be eligible to teach online and participate in mock interviews. Interns are paid a one-time stipend of $800 for completing the program and are then eligible to be hired by the college. The program is open to all candidates who are authorized to work in the United States, meet the minimum qualifications for teaching in their discipline, and have not had any paid college teaching experience.

This is just one example of an intern program designed to mentor new instructors at the college. Other colleges that offer similar programs are:

- Glendale City College
- South Orange County Community College District
- Los Rios Community College District

Check your area for similar programs.

CHAPTER 10
ACADEMIC SEARCH AND HIRING COMMITTEES

HIRING COMMITTEES IN academia are typically diverse, coming from a wide variety of disciplines. For example, to hire a full-time criminal justice instructor, it is common for the committee to consist of at least one discipline expert (administration of justice instructor) and others from different disciplines or closely related disciplines, such as sociology and paralegal studies. The committee will consist of maybe four full-time faculty members, one administrator—typically a dean—and one compliance officer whose job is to make sure that the process is fair for all candidates.

Committee members review applications to first see if candidates meet minimum qualifications and then if they meet desirable qualifications. Those scoring the highest will be invited to a first interview with the committee. I saw many applications that were missing the required documents or materials. Hiring committees often disqualify candidates for submitting incomplete applications.

For part-time instructor positions, the hiring committee composition varies. As I discussed earlier, sometimes directors or department chairs have the authority to hire without a formal interview or application; a simple resume can suffice. Other schools may have a formal hiring committee with multiple members.

The next chapter will look at the application process for an instructor position and what to expect during the interview.

CHAPTER 11

THE APPLICATION AND JOB INTERVIEW FOR AN INSTRUCTOR POSITION

TO HIRE FOR a part-time position at some institutions, the department might simply call someone who has submitted a resume and ask them for an informal interview. Based on the interview, the department might hire them to start teaching a class.

In other cases, the department or college will have applicants for a part-time position apply online where they join a pool of candidates. The department chair or their designee selects candidates from this pool to interview.

Going through pools of applicants takes time. Before inviting someone to interview, the department chair must review the application and verify that the applicant meets the minimum qualifications for the position. I can tell you from experience that many applicants do not meet the minimum qualifications based on state requirements. A pool might contain over one hundred applications. To increase the chances of getting an interview, my suggestion is to apply online and then send a greeting card or brief letter to the department chair or director of the program letting them know you have submitted an application and meet the minimum requirements and, if applicable, the desirable qualifications as well. This can save the department chair valuable time going through the pool looking for someone to interview for an assignment.

Interviews are typically structured and may include a teaching demonstration. Some do not. My best advice would be to prepare as if you were going to apply for a full-time position with the college. Those are structured processes, which I will describe below:

The department has decided to hire a full-time instructor. The College creates a job announcement, and it posts for six weeks.

Applicants are required to apply online and are expected to submit any of the following:

Resume or CV

Cover Letter

Unofficial transcripts from all schools attended

Verification of Employment letter

Three references

It is important to remember that colleges and universities will typically reject any incomplete applications. Over the years, I have seen many outstanding applicants who are refused an interview because their applications were incomplete.

After years of serving on numerous academic hiring committees for both administration of justice and other disciplines, here are the most common mistakes that typically disqualify applicants from getting an interview:

- Incomplete application package (missing transcripts, cover letters, resumes, or references); and
- No details on resume or cover letter about previous professional experience or teaching experience.

After the deadline to file, the college will create a hiring committee to review applications and conduct the first round of interviews.

Once the committee decides who to interview, invitations are sent with the date and time of the interview. Candidates are often asked to give a teaching demonstration on given a topic for ten to fifteen minutes.

On the day of the interview, the committee will ask the candidate a series of questions about the position.

Below are samples of questions an interview panel might ask:

- Please briefly summarize your qualifications for this position and explain why you are interested in becoming an administration of justice instructor.
- How do you assess student learning or what techniques do you use in the classroom to increase student learning for diverse populations?
- Please discuss strategies that you use to support diverse students who may be struggling academically in your courses.
- How do you ensure regular and effective contact among students when teaching online? Be specific about how you engage students with technology.
- Describe a difficult situation with a student, employee, or colleague and explain how you resolved it, what you learned in the process, and what you would do differently the next time.
- Describe what strategies and techniques you would use to engage students in your class and improve retention.
- Describe briefly your experience in working with students from diverse educational, socio-economic, cultural, disabilities, and ethnic backgrounds. Please then share your thoughts on how faculty members can help a diverse student population succeed.

The teaching demonstration is a critical part of the interview and can make or break a job offer. On too many occasions, candidates teach their lessons using only PowerPoint and do it badly—simply reading from the slides. Others include so much text on each slide that they are difficult to read. I'm sure you have sat through more than enough PowerPoint presentations where instructors just read from the slides, which are heavy with text. From my experience, most folks present PowerPoints poorly. PowerPoint slides should be used to spark discussion about a given topic, not act as a handout on the projector screen.

If you need to brush up on your PowerPoint presentation skills, an excellent source is *Slide:Ology: The Art and Science of Creating Great Presentations* by Nancy Duarte.

In addition, more skillful presentations implement different instructional techniques, like using the whiteboard or chalkboard, flip charts, or handouts. A great source for delivering great presentations is *Presentation Zen: Simple Ideas on Presentation Design and Delivery* by Garr Reynolds.

When you receive your interview invitation, the hiring committee might tell you what equipment will be available for the teaching demonstration. If not, make sure to bring all the items that might be needed, including a laptop computer, a flash drive, dry-erase markers, a small portable flipchart, or any handouts to distribute to committee members.

During the teaching demonstration, get the interview panelists involved. They will often tell the applicant during the teaching demonstration to treat them as if they were students. Get them involved in discussions and answering questions. Bring a small clock to keep track of time. With technology, what can go wrong, will go wrong. Bring a hard copy of any PowerPoint slides you want to present.

Within a few days after the interview, the committee will notify applicants about their decisions.

If you are selected, congratulations! Human Resources will ask you to submit personnel documents, which may include a Verification of Employment letter from your job, a TB test, and a Live Scan. If not selected, ask a committee member for feedback on your interview. Some interview panel members might be allowed to share feedback, and some might not.

CHAPTER 12

QUICK TIPS FOR LANDING AN INSTRUCTOR POSITION

Earn a degree

EARNING A DEGREE is the first step to land any type of college or university job. Even though you might be certified as the greatest trainer of all time in your full-time position, colleges and universities will not hire you without a degree. Try to earn the highest degree possible. Some colleges pay more for applicants with Master's Degrees and doctorates. Make sure that the institution where you are earning your degree is fully accredited and that course credit transfers from one institution to another. Always talk with a counselor to verify.

Become a trainer at work

Start volunteering to conduct training sessions at your place of employment.

Join instructor trade associations

Many trade associations provide teaching opportunities at annual conferences and a chance to network with other instructors.

Become an Advisory Board Member

Becoming an advisory board member is a great chance to meet decision-makers in criminal justice departments and network with other professionals.

Get certified to teach online

Create opportunities to teach across the country.

Teach noncredit CTE courses

Many of these types of classes are one- or two-day courses in a variety of different subjects.

Volunteer to be a guest speaker

Talk with department chairs and volunteer your services to speak at different criminal justice classes in your field of expertise.

Work as an intern

Apply for college teaching internships.

Rehearse your teaching demo for the interview

Rehearse your presentation to make a great impression and demonstrate your confidence and expertise. Filming yourself with a video camera on a tripod is a great tool to review your presentation. A quick ten-minute teaching demonstration captured on video will reveal strengths and weaknesses that you might not be aware of. Review the video and make the necessary corrections.

In my department, we use a checklist when evaluating part-time instructors as a reminder of what to watch for during an instructor's class.

Instructor Classroom Observation Tool

Instructor Name _____ Rater _____ Date_____

Criteria	Above average	Average	Needs Improvement
Visual Contact			
Looked at ALL students by slowly scanning			
Avoided focusing on one student or side of room			
Maintained eye contact for at least 3 seconds per person			
Did not constantly look at floor, ceiling, back of room			
Only glanced at notes (did not read directly)			
Vocal Qualities			
Maintained an even pace, using pauses well			
Varied tone and volume to maintain interest or emphasize points			
Avoided a monotone, soft, muffled voice, too fast or slow pace			
Controlled nervous responses in voice and breathing			
Avoided pause fillers (uh, um, you know, oh kay)			
Movement			
Gained and held attention and included entire audience			
Avoided distracting movements (shifting, pacing, swinging arms, jingling hands in pockets)			
Maintained an open, relaxed stance (no stiffness or barriers)			
Avoided turning back on audience (consistently faced class)			
Avoided using items as a crutch or "podium"			
Moved around the room to reduce the physical distance between instructor and students			
Gestures			
Used natural and spontaneous gestures to maintain attention			
Avoided immobilizing hands for long periods (behind back, on hips, in pockets, at sides, in front clutching cards/notes)			
Use of Training/Instructional Aids			
Used a variety of training aids to support instruction (flip chart, white board, overhead projector)			
Included use of audio or video materials to support instruction			
PowerPoint used only as part of the interactive method			
Methods of Instruction			
Used a variety of interactive methods to deliver instruction			
Used creative and unique ideas to engage the audience			
Gives examples, illustrations or applications to clarify abstract concepts			
Questioning Skills			
Periodically asks students open-ended questions to determine knowledge of topic			
Summarized key concepts from previous class			
Smooth transitions from one topic to another			
Engaged students in the instruction at least 3-6 times			
Assessment			
Used at least one assessment tool during class to evaluate student learning			
Additional Comments:			

Create a YouTube Teaching demonstration video

You sometimes don't need to wait for an invitation to do a teaching demonstration. Why not create a YouTube video teaching demonstration and send the link to prospective employers? For a teaching demonstration for an online course, select your favorite class or topic to teach and create a slide pack. If it is going to be you on the screen narrating a lecture, make sure you have proper lighting, ideally with lighting coming from the side and front of your face. Invest in a good quality microphone and webcam and position it to where you are looking directly into the camera. There are several platforms to record videos in academia including Zoom, Screencast-O-Matic, or ScreenFlow. If you use Zoom, simply have a meeting with yourself and record. Lightly edit the file and then upload to YouTube. You might want to create your own YouTube channel and upload the file to a private link.

A YouTube video of an in-person teaching demonstration is ideal for a recruiter as it lets them see how you interact with the material, students in class, handling questions, disruptions, etc. Have someone in the back of the room film and use a remote wireless microphone. A 15-minute video file is all you need.

Upload to YouTube in your private YouTube channel and send the link to interested parties.

CONCLUSION

I hope I have sparked an interest to consider a second career teaching administration of justice classes at colleges and universities. It is a second career that can serve you well not just while working a day job but also well into retirement.

In this line of work, passing on knowledge and education to the next generation along with ethical standards to uphold and support our criminal justice system is imperative. Over the years, the system has changed significantly—from the way we offer bail, to how probation and parole are granted, to policing practices and correctional policies. It is important to educate students the impact these changes make in our society and how we can learn from them. Criminal justice professionals are in a unique position to teach them and share their experiences. What better way to educate students than to have practitioners skilled in teaching to help them along the way.

Being a college instructor provides a sense of giving back to the community and making our world a much better place.

Think of a time when you were in school and a teacher inspired you to do your best and make something out of your life. What a difference that can make!

Now go teach!

GLOSSARY

Academic Affairs: A division of the college or university that oversees instruction.

Academic year: The period when students attend colleges and universities for classes, usually beginning in late August or early September and ending in June.

Adjunct: A part-time instructor or professor.

Advisory Board: A group of people that reviews an academic program of study and makes recommendations for improvement.

Assignment: A class that is assigned to an instructor.

Asynchronous class: A class that is taught 100 percent online.

Blackboard: A learning platform used for online courses.

Canvas: A learning platform used for online courses.

Credit: College credit awarded to students after completing a class.

CTE: Career Technical Education.

Curriculum Vitae: Similar to a resume and lists work history related to teaching practices.

Dual Enrollment course: A college course taught at a high school.

Hybrid class: A class that is taught in at least two different modalities, such as a class that meets half the time in person and the other half online.

Lecturer: Part-time instructor at a university.

Moodle: A learning platform used for online courses.

Noncredit: College classes that are not awarded credit toward a degree or some certificates.

Pedagogy: The methods or practices that instructors or professors implement to teach their classes.

Perkins Act: A federal act established to improve career-technical education programs, integrate academic and career-technical instruction, serve special populations, and meet gender equity needs.

Resume: A document listing all work history and education.

Seniority List: Part-time instructors who have taught a certain number of classes within a certain time frame are placed on a seniority list that gives them rights to future assignments.

Student Learning Outcomes (SLOs): Specific skills, knowledge, and abilities that students should attain after finishing a course of study.

Syllabus: A document given to students on the first day of class that lists important details about the class, expectations, schedule, assignments, and instructor information.

Synchronous class: A class that is taught in real-time with instructors and students meeting online from different locations, such as a class that is taught on Zoom.

WEBSITES

www.flexjobs.com FlexJobs. A website listing hundreds of jobs in academia across the United States and foreign countries. A paid subscription is required to view listings.

www.theiai.org International Association for Identification. This site contains job listings in forensic science and criminal investigation

www.acjs.org Academy of Criminal Justice Sciences. This site contains job listings for criminal justice instructors at colleges and universities.

https://onlinenetworkofeducators.org California Community Colleges Virtual Campus Online Network of Educators. This is a Canvas Certification training website.

https://www.cccregistry.org/jobs/index.aspx California Community Colleges Registry. This site contains job listings across California for both full-time and part-time positions.

https://www.chronicle.com The Chronicle of Higher Education. This site contains job listings for all faculty positions across the United States, including administration of justice.

https://acue.org/ The Association of College and University Educators. This is an excellent association that offers training classes on how to be a college professor. It has lots of free downloadable handouts on best practices in teaching in-person and online.

https://www.ileeta.org/ International Law Enforcement Educators and Trainers Association. ILEETA is a fraternal association of professional trainers and educators dedicated to the continuing improvement of the effectiveness of criminal justice practitioners.

https://www.iadlest.org/ The International Association of Directors of Law Enforcement Standards and Training. This site provides instructor development courses and certifications.

ADDITIONAL RESOURCES

1. Angelo, T. & Cross, P. (1993) *Classroom Assessment Techniques: A Handbook for College Teachers.* Second Edition, Jossey-Bass Publishing San Francisco, Ca. **This excellent book provides assessment techniques that can be applied to training and teaching.**

2. Brown, P. Roediger, H. McDaniel, M. (2014) *Make it Stick.* Harvard University Press. Cambridge, Massachusetts. **This is an excellent book on how educators and trainers can make learning stick into long-term memory.**

3. California Community Colleges Chancellor's Office. *Minimum Qualifications for Faculty and Administrators in California Community Colleges.* 17th edition, 2022. **This book describes the minimum academic and professional qualifications to teach vocational college courses, such as administration of justice.**

4. Duarte, N. (2008). Slide:Ology: *The Art and Science of Creating Great Presentations.* O'Reilly Media. Sebastopol, California. **This book describes in great detail how instructors can improve Power-Point presentations and think like a designer.**

5. Fink, D. (2003) *Creating Significant Learning Expe-*

riences: An Integrated Approach to Designing College Courses. Jossey-Bass Publishing San Francisco, CA. **This is an overview of how to design courses.**

6. Reynolds, G. (2012). *Presentation Zen: Simple Ideas on Presentation Design and Delivery.* New Riders, California. **This is an excellent book on presentation design and delivery.**

7. Lucas, R. (2000) *The Big Book of Flip Charts.* McGraw Hill, New York. **This is a comprehensive book on the many uses of flip charts in presentations.**

8. Allitt, P. *Art of Teaching: Best Practices from a Master Educator.* The Great Courses. *https://www.thegreatcourses.com/* **This is an overall introduction to teaching.**